Bloom

Bloom

A Gift For The Girl Learning To Love Her Beautiful Soul

SHANI JAY

THOUGHT CATALOG Books
BROOKLYN, NY

THOUGHT CATALOG Books

 Designed by KJ Parish. Cover photography by © Boonsom

Published by Thought Catalog Books, a division of The Thought & Expression Co., Williamsburg, Brooklyn. Founded in 2010, Thought Catalog is a website and imprint dedicated to your ideas and stories. We publish fiction and non-fiction from emerging and established writers across all genres. For general information and submissions: manuscripts@thoughtcatalog.com.

Second edition, 2017

ISBN: 978-1945796524

Printed and bound in the United States.

10 9 8 7 6 5 4 3 2 1

Dad & Mum, for always imparting your wisdom and guidance to me and for your unwavering love and support since day one.

Ravi, for not only being a brother but a best friend, too.

Sam, for being there when this book was all just in my mind and believing I could get to here.

And for all of the girls who need a little reminder today to love themselves. x

Feel your petals grow
restless as you
become sure of
what you hold within.
As you grow in
confidence and soak
up the sunlight.
Allow your true colours to
burst open from their bud,
showering your magic.

Bloom and blossom.

Contents

Introduction

Growing up as a girl in our world today is harder than it ever has been. The intense peer pressure, impossible beauty standards, and the uncontrollable need to be everything to everyone has left us with little or no love left for ourselves.

Bloom is a heartfelt collection of writing for the girls and women who are struggling to love themselves. If you're looking for a guide to self-love, an instant confidence boost, or comforting reassurance that you are most certainly not alone in your feelings, *Bloom* was written for you.

Because the truth is—I used to walk in your shoes. I used to be that girl who woke up in the morning and didn't want to get out of bed. I felt ugly, alone, devastatingly unhappy, and uninspired by my life. I didn't love myself, and I had absolutely no idea how or where to begin.

But I want you to know that it gets better. I promise, it does. Everyone has the power within them to embark on a magical journey of self-love. Today, you'll find me a completely transformed young woman because of the people, the books, and the positive messages I consistently choose to surround myself with.

Bloom will show you that through the power of self-love, the life you've always dreamed of living is right there ready for the taking. Allow the words you read to sink in and become your truth. You'll realise those happy, glowing, have-it-all-made girls you see can be you. You, as much as anybody, deserve a beautiful life, overflowing with love.

Don't wait until tomorrow to start loving yourself. Don't wait for somebody to walk into your life and tell you you're worthy. Choose to love yourself today.

The book you're about to read will be the beginning of a beautiful new life. One filled with an abundance of love, happiness, and self-worth. All you have to do is keep reading and allow your heart to be open.

For more sunshine and positive vibes, you can join The Glow Getter Tribe (shanijay.com/glowgetter) for free today and take part in The 7 Day Self-Love Sanctuary!

Love, Shani x

1

To The Girls Who Need To Remember To Love Themselves

This is for all of the girls out there who have ever woken up to a new morning's sunrise and felt like they don't want to get out of bed because they don't measure up. The girls who have wished that they could wake up as someone else for a day…anyone else. The girls who feel like they're somehow less than what they should be. The girls who don't even know how to begin loving themselves. This is for all of you who have been led to believe that your beautiful souls are not *enough.*

Not pretty enough. Not smart enough. Not popular enough. Not hard working enough. Not talented enough. Not thin enough. Not curvy enough. Not loud enough. Not mellow enough. Not brave enough. Not funny enough. Not experienced enough. Not innocent enough.

Never enough.

Have you ever woken up in the morning not knowing who you are? Why you're here? What is the point of all this, anyway?

Well, I have. More times than I care to remember. We're all just fragile human beings, carrying breakable hearts and more feelings than we know what to do with. **Sometimes, we're *all* a little unsure.** The truth is, we all will have our great days and our not-so-rosy ones. No woman wakes up every single day feeling incredible about herself; that's simply not reality. That being said, the good days should, without question, kick more ass than the crappy days.

I've come to realise that the most genuinely beautiful women who grace this earth are the ones who believe that they are. They don't give a damn what anyone else thinks because they realise that the only person they truly need to impress is themselves. And that thinking in itself is where your true beauty can be found. It can't be found in the pages of that self-help book, or in the shower of compliments from the cute guy you met in the club on Saturday night, or in the eyes of your partner whose unwavering adoration for you radiates through.

You were always meant to be your own saviour all along.

Please don't be the girl who waits for some guy you barely know to come along and tell you you're beautiful before you start believing it. He might stick around, and he might not; either way, he does not have the power to change how you truly feel about yourself, deep down. **Not really. No one does.**

You are what you believe. You are the voices in your head that you choose to listen to or disregard. You are as good as you allow yourself to be. You are anything you dare to dream possible.

You are the only person who has the choice, each day, to wake up and decide that you *are* beautiful.

The choice, if you're feeling a little bruised, to get up anyway. To blast your happy song as loud as you please, sing along to it with everything you've got while taking a glorious invigorating shower; to pick out your favourite summer dress and apply that bold scarlet red lipstick like you mean it. The choice to make yourself feel better, the choice to get up and keep moving forward, to keep choosing yourself.

If no one told you that you're beautiful today, I want you to look at the reflection staring back at you in the nearest mirror, and tell that girl she is beautiful. Be sure to say it like you mean it. Your freckle clusters, your corner-of-the-eye creases, those gappy teeth, or your slightly off-centre nose. Your child-bearing hips, your invisible thigh gap, or those slightly-wider-than-you'd-like ankles. All those parts of you that you believe to be flaws, only appear that way because you've been *convinced* to view them in that light. Think of them as your beauty spots. They make you, you. Why would you want to try and be anybody else? Don't compare yourself to a hot stranger on Instagram. Don't hate the girl you think is your competition, because she's really just a *soul sister* in disguise. The world already has a beautiful her, and her, and her… what it doesn't have yet is a beautiful you.

You harbour more potential and possibility and greatness within you than you can even begin to *imagine* right now. You hold a gift that is unique to you—no one will possess the same one; not now, not ever. And in knowing this, how could you wish to not be *you?*

How could you not believe in that incredible woman that you see staring back at you?

You may not be able to see it right now, but you have your very own one-off flavour of sparkle. And your sparkle has more than enough light to shine fiercely all on its own. You simply have to find it, continue to fuel it, and never allow it to go out.

Feeling beautiful will always begin, and end, with *you*.

2

Read This When You're Wondering When Things Will Finally Get Better

I wish I could tell you it gets better.

But it doesn't.

Like Joan Rivers said, "It doesn't get better. You get better."

As the sun sets upon each day, you will have learned, you will have grown, and you will have changed. Maybe not a lot, but at least a little.

You become resilient. You get pushed down, and you jump right back up. You take every no, every rejection, every setback, on your chin and keep fighting on in pursuit of all the yeses you know lie ahead of you, patiently waiting for you to reach out and grab them with both hands.

You will learn to be less sensitive. This might be harder for you than most. But you will eventually understand not to take everything as a bullet aimed at your sweet heart. Because you'll come to realise that nothing other people do is because of you, it is because of themselves. Don't lose your sensitive soul completely, though—it's most certainly a gift to feel so deeply in a way that others can't begin to imagine.

You grow stronger.

This might happen quietly, little by little, until one day you take a step back and have a careful look at yourself. And you'll see it. You'll see the huge leaps forward you have made from where you once were. And you'll think to yourself, *Wow, I did that.* Because you never knew you had that kind of strength residing in you all along. But trust me, it was there.

You will grow wiser. If you pay close attention, every day has a blessing or a lesson waiting for you. You just have to open your heart to it. Make mistakes, learn from them, try not to make the same mistake again. Be forgiving; do your best to forget. Sometimes you won't and you shouldn't. Other times you must.

You finally begin to realise your worth. So fiercely that no one on the planet could drag you back down to feeling worthless ever again. You realise the true measure of worth comes from within you, only you, and is not dependent on anyone else's beliefs. You won't be ruled by others; you belong to yourself.

You will finally understand that you own your worth.

You become a fucking wolf. A lion. A warrior. You stop taking people's shit. You stand up; you stand with pride and finally take on the starring role in the epic show that is your life. You no longer make apologies for who you are and what you believe in. You have BIG love for that person, and screw anyone who doesn't match that—you no longer need or want validation. You're not done yet, though. *No.* Every day is a new opportunity to become an even better version of yesterday's you. And you're not prepared to waste a single one.

I wish I could tell you it gets better. It doesn't. **But I know that you do.**

3

You Deserve To Love Yourself Unapologetically

No one can champion you quite like your own self can. No one wants you to succeed half as much as you do. No one fully knows your story: where you have been, the place you find yourself in now, and where you hope to go next.

It's always game time. Be prepared. Practice hard, much harder than you think you'll need to perform. Be sure to turn up, early and to every single game, even to those games you may think don't matter. Be present in all of your moments. **Cheer loudly.** Do not give a second thought to anyone who may be listening and judging from the sidelines.

Support yourself even when you meet with failure—maybe a little extra than you usually would. Don't even think for a second about switching teams; this is the only team you were destined to cheer for from the day you were given life. When you give your all, but your opposition proves to be a little too tough, do not give up. Promise yourself to come back stronger, and fight even harder the next time around. Celebrate even the smallest of wins. But don't settle for those.

Always believe there are bigger and better triumphs to be had ahead.

You are not merely a winner, you are a champion, a warrior, and a fighter. Get on out there and shower the world with your sparkling magic.

The truth is that no one in this world will ever have your back like you do. And no one is going to believe in you and your talent half as much as you can.

If you don't believe you're fucking awesome, who the hell else will?

The power to become the person you've always wanted to be rests quietly within you. You must go on the journey to seek it out. You don't need to search elsewhere; look inwards. Everything you need has been there for all this time. But you have to believe it. You have to believe in yourself. **You have to drown out those little voices in your head telling you that *you can't do anything spectacular because you'll fail*, or *because you're simply not good enough*, and *what on earth makes you think that you have what it takes*?** Pay no attention to this. Hear those voices and make it your mission to knock them flat out with your brilliance.

Don't waste the magic with which you have been graciously gifted. It won't wait around for you forever.

4

This Is Why You're So Hard On Yourself (And Why You Shouldn't Be)

You are your own harshest critic. You find yourself saying cruel and unkind words to yourself, words that you would never *dream* of voicing to anyone else. You apply constant pressure and gradually increase the weight over time. And you can't see it now, but you're slowly crushing yourself into the ground.

You're so damn hard on yourself, and you don't know how to stop.

Because there's always a girl who's smarter, or prettier, or more popular than you are. Always someone in front or above you, leaving you breathless behind in their trail of dust. There's always someone a little further ahead on their journey. There's always a reason for you to believe you aren't quite *enough*.

Because you're convinced you have to do *everything* in this life and be everything to everyone, all at once. Because you've been taught to be a yes girl, and **no** is profanity you must not use in your vocabulary. Because yes pleases others, and so yes is what we must say to get ahead.

Because the world is filled with **garbage.** Celebrity obsession, gossip magazines, TV shows, clothing, and makeup by the bucket-load, all designed to tell you what you should look like. What you should be interested in. How you should dress. The colour of your hair. And the width of your waistline. A full set of makeup that covers your flaws while still giving you that totally fake 'natural' look. Not too much skin on show but just enough so you don't look like a prude. Longer eyelashes, bigger boobs, fuller lips, thicker eyebrows, glossier hair, and on and on. It doesn't end. All dictating who you should aspire to be instead of celebrating the incredible girl you already are.

Because it's all too easy to let our mistakes cloud over us and shadow all of our success. It's easy to focus on what we're not instead of all that we are. And we've been led to criticise, to analyse, and to continually mould ourselves into someone 'desirable' to others.

Because you think you have to be *perfect*. You think that failing will automatically label you a failure. And so you're scared to even try. You're scared to go after what you want. You're hard on yourself for even thinking for a second that you *could*.

Because someone along the way told you you weren't good enough. You weren't worthy. You weren't beautiful. You weren't *wanted*. **And it breaks my heart that you decided to believe them.** You allowed your worth to be dictated by a *nobody*.

And even now that nobody is gone, those feelings of being not enough stick around like a Band-Aid begging to be ripped off.

Because people continually enter us females into competition with one another. A competition none of us ever willingly agreed to. We're so hard on ourselves because we can't stop sizing up the girl beside us, calculating if we're better than her or not. *They* don't want us to know it, but through cheering each other on, and being happy for one another's success, we would be far stronger than we are alone.

You're so hard on yourself because of everything that has happened to you up to this point. Every time someone put you down and every time you didn't stand up for yourself. Every time you said yes when your mind was screaming no. Every time someone else's dreams came true while yours remained unfulfilled in your mind. Every time you stumbled. And every time you were scarred.

You're so used to being this hard on yourself you don't know how to *stop*.

5

13 Reasons Why It Totally Rocks To Be A Girl Today

1. It's the age of the GIRL SQUAD.

Sisters coming together and doing it for themselves. We've finally realised the importance of building each other up instead of trying to tear each other down, and we're putting it into practice more than ever. We now compete with, and challenge, ourselves to be better with each new day, month, and year.

2. We have so many inspirational role models.

Queens like Oprah, Malala, Emma Watson and Beyoncé are making sure we channel our inner girl power and don't accept any less than we deserve in any situation. Even though they don't know us, it feels as though they have our backs and that they're rooting for us to become the best possible versions of ourselves, cheering us on the whole way. Their battles aren't their own; they're our battles too.

3. We also know some great men.

Men who realise that there shouldn't be a hierarchy between us and that all people deserve the same respect, the same attention, and the same opportunities as one another. Men who have and will continue to champion us all the way.

4. We have the right to vote.

If you're reading this, you're probably not one of the unlucky ones who are still waiting patiently for this justice. And I know this isn't a new revelation, but women suffered so we would have this right, and it's a downright slap in the face to waste it. I struggle to imagine how I would feel if I didn't have this right, simply for being born the 'inferior' gender.

5. We have fewer career restrictions.

Whether it's painting or writing, cooking or fixing cars, becoming a lawyer or even playing professional b-ball—anything you want to do, you can do it. It is all possible. Your grandmother will likely tell you a hugely contrasting view of her youth, compared to the endless avenues you were given access to without question.

6. Our voices will no longer be silenced or ignored.

We can all have a voice and can use that voice for good if we so choose. The world has begun to wake up and take notice of what we have to say—yes, it may take more than a few attempts on our part, but stand strong with your message, and don't ever let anyone silence or censor you.

7. We get to be selfish.

It's socially acceptable for us to finally be selfish for a little while. We can go after the career we've always dreamed of, focus on our own goals and ambitions, and our own success. We answer to no one, and we beat to the rhythm of our own drum.

8. We have time.

To explore the world and to explore ourselves. To discover what makes us tick. Find our true passions. What each of our hearts' true calling is. What we're here on this earth to accomplish. And every time we take a step back and think about the joy of this, it never fails to feel sweetly luxurious.

9. There is a lot less pressure to settle down.

I'm not saying the stigma of being 30 and single without kids has completely disappeared. But there's now so much less pressure on us to get married off and start popping out babies as if that's all we were made to do. And screw those small-minded people who still cling to these backward views.

10. We're looking after our minds and bodies.

We're eating healthier, we're working out, we're meditating, we're indulging in manis and pedis and massages, we're jetting off to explore exotic corners of the world on our own, we're wearing matching lingerie—not for anyone else but ourselves, and don't we all feel so much better for it? #ThisGirlDoes

11. We're carving out our own paths and making our mark.

We're in the age of social media stars. Fashion bloggers, beauty vloggers, youtube personalities, and self-made female CEOs of incredibly thriving new brands and companies that were created from zero. Women doing it for themselves and breaking the rules. There has never been an easier time to chase your dreams. There are no gatekeepers shutting us out anymore. Everything is yours for the taking if you work your arse off and want it badly enough.

12. We've come a helluva long way from where we started.

Though there is still much farther to go in terms of true equality, we have been given access to much of the same opportunities as men have. And this is continually being debated and kept in media focus in order to further bridge the gap. These discussions and leaps forward did not seem possible 30 years ago. You have probably witnessed a great change from when you were a child to where you find yourself standing today. We can, and we should, have it all.

13. We no longer have to pick just one role.

And we will no longer be defined as either a career woman or a mum. We can be daughters and working girls and girlfriends and wives and mothers and homemakers and go-getters. We have finally un-labelled ourselves.

6

This Is For The Girls Who Refuse To Lower Their Standards For Anyone

Has anyone ever told you your standards are too high? You don't live in the 'real' world? You expect **far too much?** Which of course means people will inevitably let you down? Because how could they *not* when you waltz around with your high hopes, your rosy glasses firmly on at all times, and your keg of principles?

I've been told this often, followed by much eye-rolling and self-defending on my part. So much so that I now let those words of others land and roll off my shoulders as if they were a couple of rogue rain droplets mistakenly falling from the sky. Here's what I have to say to all of you who ever find yourself in the same pair of shoes:

Good for you for having fucking standards.

Good for you for deciding to set your bar super high.

Good for you for not settling for mediocre, okay, average, *mehhh* that'll do, or just fine.

Many who walk this earth cannot imagine a life through your way of thinking. They can't, and they refuse to allow themselves to imagine people surprising them. Because they've only fallen short time and time again. Realise you are what you allow to happen to you. You are the behaviour you tolerate, you are—to a great extent—the people you keep around you, and you are the only person with the power to change any situation you find yourself in. If you are keeping company with someone who makes you question your faith and humanity in the world, you have to step back and ask yourself, W*hat the hell am I doing?* And it is your responsibility to comfortably distance yourself from them or eliminate them from your life completely. This is no time for *gently does it*. We are talking about your *faith* here.

People might let you down occasionally, yes. Perhaps they let you down a *lot*. Maybe every single person who has shown up so far has let you down spectacularly. But so fucking what? Why should you allow the actions of others to influence the way you choose to live your life, the way you view strangers? You absolutely shouldn't.

Never allow those who are jaded to try and jade you. Keep your head high and your expectations even higher.

Lower yourself for *no one*. If people like you and want to be in your life, they will be. It's as simple as that—don't make it complicated when it's not. Your people won't make you feel wrong for being who you fundamentally are. The people you truly want in your life are the ones who see you sitting pretty in your rose-tinted glasses and will say, "I like how you choose to see it." Though they may disagree with you, they would never dream of making your beliefs feel ridiculous.

You know what all of us optimists should do? Encourage the cynical ones to raise their standards.

To strive for better. To find their faith in people. To expect more. Don't mould yourself to fit in with other people and their standards, let them fit to yours.

Here's what you should say to the people who say your expectations are too high—I will never expect any less from others than I expect from myself.

And I expect the *world* from myself. I really hope you do, too.

7

We Owe It To Ourselves To Be This Kind Of Woman

We need to be comfortable in our own skin.

This may not come naturally to you at first, and that is okay. It might take years of conscious practise on your part to eventually feel confident and comfortable with who you really are at the very core. But take that time, and be sure to get yourself there. You owe it to your heart and your soul to honour yourself, always. And don't ever let anyone make you feel as though you won't be accepted for who you are. If you feel the need to make changes and to better yourself, please do, as long as you are making those changes for you and for nobody else.

We must be confident saying yes and saying no.

Never, ever, do anything to solely please somebody else. If saying yes makes you happy, then say it. If saying no will make you happier, then say it. Don't hesitate. If you're reading this, it's likely that you have a high level of choice and freedom in the way you lead your life and the choices you are able to make daily. You're one of the lucky ones. Don't ever willingly hand over your gift of freedom to somebody else. Compose yourself, decide what you want, and express that decision with confidence. Never feel guilty for doing what feels right or for who you are in this moment. You don't owe anyone a dime.

We need to be graceful when we are wronged.

Our defence mechanism will instinctively raise our guards and prepare us for war when we believe we are coming under attack. But as the saying goes, an eye for an eye will only end up making the whole world blind. Hitting back in anger will not undo what was done to us. And it cannot, and will not, make us feel better in the long run. Distance yourself from those who continually choose to bruise you. Don't tarnish yourself with the toxic paint from someone else's brush. You were born with the strength to rise above it. Turn the other cheek, and don't waste another precious one of your thoughts or seconds on the way others choose to behave. That is none of your business. Don't choose to make it so. Continue to carry yourself with the grace and integrity that you always have done.

We need to be kind to everybody. Always.

Kindness is possibly the most important thing of all. A true act of kindness can only come from someone who carries a good heart. Anyone can have a good heart, so long as they choose it. If ever you find yourself at rock bottom with seemingly nothing to offer, know that you will always find the gift of kindness residing within you, ready to pour out of your soul and into the lives of others. Whichever path you choose to take, be sure to be kind to everyone you meet along your way, including those who can do nothing for you. You will meet them all again, someday.

But don't forget to be kind to yourself. We are often our own worst critics and tend to dwell on mistakes and not pay nearly enough attention to all of our successes and triumphs. All of us could do with a sprinkle of kindness on each of our days. You never know the kind of day that somebody else might be having. Your words or actions might just be everything they are desperately seeking.

We need to be aware that our beauty is far more than our looks.

We know that all of our looks will begin to fade one day. We know. Yet we choose to sideline this knowledge. We place such high importance on the physical appearance of ourselves and of others, quietly knowing that it shouldn't matter, but somehow finding that is still does. We often discount the real, hidden beauty that can be found within. Ask yourself, if everybody was blind, how many people would you really impress? Start by bettering yourself from the inside, and the outside will follow in turn.

When it comes to relationships, don't make the vain mistake of choosing the person who is the most beautiful—choose the person who makes your world the most beautiful place that you can imagine. And know that the you right now is beautiful, regardless of if anyone sees your beauty or not. Just because something cannot be seen, it doesn't mean it's not there. Trust me when I tell you, people will always be able to feel it.

We need to be brave when we are scared.

The feeling of being afraid is a good one because it reminds us we are all human and not a damn single one of us is invincible. It reminds us that we are alive. It reminds us that we are so very small and fragile. Sometimes you will feel a little fragile. Maybe a whole lot fragile. But know that fear is merely a hologram, an image we conjure up ourselves from the darkest depths of our souls.

Battle your way through the fear, and confront the voices in your head that will always be there trying to convince you that you are worthless and incapable of greatness. The more times you do something, the easier it becomes. You will probably look back a year later and wonder what the hell you were so scared of in the first place. It's just life. Don't find yourself at the end of it wishing you had challenged yourself more, pushed yourself harder, worried less, and taken more risks.

We need to be happy for other women's successes.

Hating her won't make you feel or do any better. Jealousy doesn't suit you anything like happiness does. And what you need to know is that having what she has won't truly make you happy because you are not her. Her path is so very different to yours. Your needs and deepest desires are innate to you, and only you.

We need to lift each other's spirits up high, send out the warmest of wishes, and embark on our own journeys of success. When you radiate genuine kind and positive thoughts, those are what you shall receive back from the universe. Wise men and women will never enter the ring with karma. They know better.

We must be self-loving before we begin to love others.

You have to fall in love with yourself first and foremost. You need to be whole on your own. Don't purposely leave yourself incomplete, naively believing that someone else is meant to fill in your blank spaces. They cannot. They can only add to the foundations you have already built within you, but those foundations are down to you. Make them as strong and unbreakable as you can, for they will need to last you a lifetime.

Discover what excites you, and what you loathe, what turns you on, and what keeps you lying wide awake in deep thought at night. Find out who you really are because only then will you be able to see the one you are meant to be looking for. Take your time. The world will still be here, waiting. Love has no time-keepers.

We have to be our own cheerleaders.

Don't ever wait for someone to pick you up off the floor and shake you awake to your life. If you do find yourself in a time of need, be still and look inside yourself. Everything we could need will already be residing quietly within us; waiting patiently for us to seek it out. It all rests on your shoulders. Your life will be what YOU choose to make of it. Maybe you're not quite where you hoped you would be by now. But that's okay. Just keep going forward. Sometimes you will crawl, and sometimes you will fly. You are amazing; don't ever forget that. Encourage yourself. Fight hard for what you want. Believe in yourself and the message you are carrying here on this earth, for no one's message will be the same as yours.

8

This Is Life

This is life. And it won't always be fair. Sometimes, you'll have horribly rainy days. Days that a cup of tea cannot fix. Nothing will seem to go right. You'll fall out of love. It will be messy. People will screw you over. And you'll struggle to keep your faith. You'll face rejection, and an army of haters. The world will begin to feel like a scary place. You'll lose best friends. And loved ones you care deeply for. Some will be gone forever. Tears will roll down your face, and you won't be able to make them stop. You might find yourself wishing you could switch places with someone else. Anybody else. Life won't go the way you'd planned. Someone will break your heart into a million shards. Maybe you'll break theirs too. You'll find yourself lost, and alone. You'll lose hope. You'll fuck up. Multiple times. You will fall down, hitting rock bottom. And you will fail.

You will think that life couldn't possibly get any worse than it is right now.

Then you'll realise that *this is just life.* This is what you signed up for. And nothing can break you—unless you allow it to.

The truth is, you'll fall in love again. You will. But with a more careful heart. And this time it will feel right. It will be life changing. You'll make new friends. Maybe you'll make a new family too. When you find your will, you will find your way. You will begin to see that your life will be what you decide to make of it. Days are only rainy ones, if you don't create your sunshine. You will finally say no to being a victim of your own life. You'll say your goodbyes to anyone and anything toxic. You will rise up, and stand strong all on your own. And you'll be a better person for all of your strife. Each scar will hold its own special lesson. You'll learn to treasure the unexpected twists and turns that make up your unique journey here. You'll realise facing your fears is the only way to truly feel *alive*. You'll learn to trust in the timing of your life. Knowing that the universe has a way of giving you exactly what you need at the right time. Life will teach you that your existence here is fleeting. That you are not invincible, and nobody is. Every day here is nothing short of a miracle. And in knowing that, you see that miracles are not rare. For they happen *every day.*

And how could that fill you with anything but hope?

9

9 Tiny Things You Should Be Thankful For Every Day

1. Waking up.

Do you have any idea how many people have that everyday miracle silently stolen away from them in the night? Too many. And sometimes completely without warning. You woke up today. You get to have now. You're already one of the lucky ones. Believe that.

2. Fresh air.

It's easy to take something that we do more than 25,000 times a day, mostly without even thinking about it, for granted. I get that. But the next time you step outside your door, just take a minute to focus on your breathing. Take in that clean, fragrant sweetness of the green grass, variety of trees, bouquet of flowers, and the cotton clouds overhead infusing together to create that soft smell of fresh air. Just remember that while it should be like this everywhere in our world, it's not.

3. Clean running water.

You open a tap, and floods of crystal clear liquid spill out. Cooling, quenching, warming, cleansing. So simple and basic, but we continue to rely on this process day in and day out. You don't have to travel ten miles each day to find clean running water. It's right there at your fingertips. Next time you open a tap, be mindful of this.

4. Education.

Please do not take this blessing for granted. So many children have this basic right robbed from them at birth, sometimes just for being born a girl, and wish for nothing more than waking up bright and early Monday morning to begin school. Something that others of us loathe. I was guilty of this. Because, at the time, I just didn't get the big picture. Learning something new…being educated… An incredibly smart lady once said something that stuck with me forever: "Smart is sexy, and it's the only kind of sexy that lasts."

5. Your body.

How many of us are all too familiar with tearing ourselves down based on what we look like on the outside? Yep, me too. But we're forgetting just how strong each of us really are. Your legs, long or short, allow you to run to wherever you choose to go; your hands allow you to create magic through words or colour on a page; your arms allow you to stretch out wide and unite yourself with each new day; your nose, no matter what shape or size, allows you to take deep breaths in and then out. How could you not love a body that allows us to do all of these incredible things, over and over again? Learn to love the body you were given.

6. Loved ones.

Your mum, your dad, your brother, your sister, or your best friend. It doesn't matter how many you have because all you ever really need is one. One person who loves you and one person to love; that is more than enough to fill our souls with the light and warmth which they crave. So if you have just one person in your life who loves you, you are already winning. You're winning at life because what could possibly make any of us richer than giving and receiving love? In the end, love is all there will ever be.

7. Freedom.

We can say yes, and more importantly we can say no. We can choose to be artists and models and actors; we can choose a career over getting married and starting a family. We can believe in whichever higher power or choose not to believe in anything but ourselves. We can love whomever we fall in love with. You might scream, "Well of course we can!" but many people are punished simply for making any one of these choices. Be thankful that you really do have a choice.

8. Possibility.

Because who knows? Today you could write a business plan or finally begin that book. You might fall in love today. You might finally succeed at something you've been working towards, or you may even fail. Some you will choose; others will choose you. It's all so very uncertain, but that's what makes it so damn exciting, doesn't it? When you climb into bed this evening, something will have changed within you. You will have grown. You will have learned. You will be stronger than all of your yesterdays.

9. The chance to start over.

Did you make a bad choice? Did you hurt someone you love? Did you fall in love but were afraid to tell the person whom you fell in love with? Like I said, if you're one of the lucky ones, you'll wake up to a beautiful new sunrise tomorrow, a new beginning where everything starts from zero again. And you will have the chance to do anything that you choose. Anything. You just have to decide to start.

10

I Am Not An I Don't Give A Fuck Kind Of Girl

I'm not an IDGAF kind of girl.

I'm not convinced I ever will be. Sometimes I wish I was. Life seems easier when it's black and white, take me or leave me, but either way, don't try and fuck with me. I used to imagine myself one day buying an 'I DON'T GIVE A FUCK' slogan tee and owning it down the street without being ironic. But the truth is that I give a fair amount of fucks. I'm a sensitive soul and for the most part, *I care.*

I care when I'm on the way to work and pass a homeless, helpless guy in the street. I care if my friend thinks I'm being a shit friend. I care if I ever unknowingly hurt your feelings. I care if I'm texting some guy I barely know non-stop, and suddenly he decides he's going to cut communication without an explanation. I care if I make a careless mistake and it has real consequences for someone else. I care if someone I love is having a tough time, and I can't melt that pain away.

Here's the deal—I really don't give a fuck that I care about all of those things.

I *like* the fact I don't want to bring pain to other people's lives. I like the fact I want to succeed so much so I feel every rejection at heart-level, no matter how trivial it may seem on the outside looking in. I like how I feel everything deeply in a way others cannot. I like that I care because I pride myself on being the best version of myself that I can be, and to me that means being someone who allows themselves to be vulnerable, to feel hurt, address it, and then recover stronger than before. It would be a much easier life if I hand-on-heart did not give a fuck about any of the above. But easy is not living to the fullest.

I don't give a fuck if you don't like me, don't believe in me, or don't want to be with me. But do you *really* think that means it hurts any less when you call someone names and try to beat them down? That it hurts any less being told by someone you're never going to be successful in your chosen career? Or that it hurts any less when the person you love announces they have fallen out of love with you? I don't believe I need to begin to tell you how much all of that fucking *hurts.* Everyone has been there. Everyone has experienced their share of rejection, loss, and pain. So everyone understands the power certain experiences hold to devastate and rip you apart on the inside.

Even if you wear some of the thickest skin, you are not invincible to all of the world's pain. Nobody is.

I give *so many fucks,* and I want you to know it's okay if you do too.

It's okay to feel compassion and to care about problems that are not your own. It's okay if something or someone hurts you and you end up acknowledging some of that pain. It's more than okay if you're not the guy or girl who is able to let everything ping-pong off you, barely even noticing as it does. Allow yourself to feel hurt if you do, but don't ever allow that hurt to stay. It doesn't belong inside you.

We've been sold this ridiculous notion that not giving a fuck means you're *stronger*—that you're a warrior who takes no shit and you're a total BOSS. I see it differently. **How can you pour your blood, sweat, and tears into *anything* while simultaneously 'not giving a fuck'?** Screw the haters, but you have to *care*. Don't convince yourself that you don't.

Never be all out of fucks to give.

11

If You're Not In Love With Your Life, Change It

If you're not in love with your life, *change it.*

If ever you should wake up and find yourself on the wrong path, get off. If you're in a relationship with someone who keeps hurting your heart, leave. If you hate your job that damn much and can't stop telling everyone so, quit. If you live in a town that has gotten too small, find someplace new to explore. If the woman you are today falls short of who that little girl imagined you'd be, start making her proud. If you find yourself unsure of the person staring back at you in the mirror, it's time to start soul searching. If you feel like you're living your life on somebody else's terms, *stop*. Stop now. Before you become too bitter and too jaded—before you lose all hope in this world and all faith in *yourself.*

If you're not in love with your life, change it.

If the world has become a scary place to you, it's time to rise up and face your fears. If the reality of being a grown-up has begun to weigh heavily on your shoulders, stand up and become stronger. If everyone you know and love has turned their back on you, *please* try your best not to fall apart. If the one you love breaks your heart, remember you will mend in time. When you feel your soul slipping away, hold on and *don't let go.* **And if you're struggling to find a reason to keep going, whatever you do, don't stop looking until you find one.**

If you're not in love with your life, change it.

Stop spending your precious time and energy on things that bring you no joy. Start doing more of what makes you happy. Those passions and people and pastimes that make you come alive. Maybe you haven't found what that is yet And that's okay. But spend time trying new things so you move closer each day to discovering your soul's work. Never accept the hand you've been dealt, and don't just wait around for life to happen to you or pass you by. **Wake up and realise you are responsible for your own happiness.** Don't depend on anyone else for that. **Start owning it.** Find something that makes you want to leap out of that cosy bed before the sun even blinks in the morning.

If you're not in love with your life, promise me you'll do whatever it takes to fall in love with it again. **Because this life really is beautiful if only you give it the chance to be.** If only you realise what you give will come back to you in abundance. If only you realise that in order to find and experience true love, you must discover it within *your* heart first.

Take control of your life. Live it; live it extraordinarily well. And be sure to fall head over heels in love with it.

After all, it's never too late to become the person you hope to be.

12

It's Funny How Things Don't Work Out (And Funny How They Always Do)

It's funny how things don't work out. *It's funny how they do.*

Funny how we spend so much time worrying and stressing over all the unimportant parts of our lives—our work and money—and we turn a blind eye to the truly important, finite things like our time and our loved ones.

Isn't it funny how some of us manage to make all our dreams a beautiful alternate reality, yet some of us never even come close to experiencing the taste of success?

It's funny how the one person you think you're certain of can disappoint you dearly and the one you're so unsure of can surprise you in ways you never imagined.

Funny how your heart can shatter so terribly that you can't see it ever mending, so messily that you swear off loving again. But then someone waltzes into your life unexpectedly and makes you want to risk your heart all over again.

It's funny how you lived alone for so long, quite content with your own company, and had pretty much given up hope of finding your person, so you don't even realise it at first when you do set eyes on them.

Isn't it funny how your whole life can literally change in a second, without any warning? It's funny how you either choose to adjust yourself to that change or refuse it and reside in denial.

It's funny how separately, each one of our choices seems insignificant, but then you start to piece them together and you see that each one was leading you a little closer towards your destiny.

Funny how you can wait your whole damn life for the perfect person and then one day it suddenly hits you that there is no perfect person. 'The One' is simply the one you decide to make yours, forever.

And isn't it funny how we can carelessly promise each other forever only to leave shortly after? Yet some of us manage to make it all the way to forever.

It's funny how some things don't work out.

It's funny how they do.

13

This Is How You Must Promise To Love Me

Promise you will love me with each new sunrise, every breath you take, and the entirety of your heart.

Promise me that we'll always make time for each other and to celebrate the one of a kind love that we together have made.

Promise that you won't give me half of you, because I am a girl who wants to see and know and love all of you. Even the parts you're not so keen on yourself. *Especially* those parts. Because I want you to know that our flaws and crazy quirks are the very things that make us so beautifully human.

Promise that you'll make me *feel* it. That you'll make your love known. I know it's hard. It's hard to bare your soul to anyone. It's incredibly hard for me, too. But promise at least to try.

Promise not to take us for granted. Promise to nurture and to work on our love always. Without this, we will cease to grow. Our love will stand still.

Promise me you'll continue to try. Because that's what it takes to not fall back out of love with someone. You both have to work at it to keep things exciting. It won't work if one person is not putting in the same amount of care and attention.

Promise me that you won't choose to give up on us. Even when you feel like everything is falling apart and you don't believe that I'll be able to help you stick any of it back together.

Promise to practice forgiveness because it's inevitable we'll both say and do things sometimes that we do not mean or wish we could take back. But we can't. All we can do is continue to move forward, together.

For two will always be stronger than one.

Promise that you'll look into my eyes when you ask me if I'm okay and that you won't always believe me when I tell you that I am. I'm the kind of girl who doesn't want to burden anyone with my troubles. But sometimes it's nice to share them with you. I'd really like that. I would.

Promise me that when it gets tough you'll fight for us because I promise you that I will. Always. This was never going to be easy. Know that nothing worth having ever is. But for me, we're worth the blood, the sweat, and all of the tears that come with choosing a forever kind of love. The kind that all of us are searching and praying for.

Promise to love me if I hit rock bottom. When I pull away and try to distance myself from your love. When I do whatever I can to tear everything we've built right back down to rubble on the ground. When I'm hurting from a pain so intense that I can no longer hear my own thoughts circling in my head. Promise to stick by my side and know that I will do the same for you.

Promise me that if you're truly, madly, deeply in love with me, you won't let go.

But promise me that if you ever find your eyes or your heart wandering that you'll muster the courage to explain yourself. If you don't plan to love me like I'm everything, then please let me go. Let me go now. Set me free; allow me to fly. Let me find the man that will look at me each day like I'm *fairy dust*. Let me find him. Because our time here is fleeting, and we all deserve our shot at a love like that.

And if you plan on breaking your promises, please promise me nothing. Don't ever say something you know you don't mean. I would rather bear the temporary pain of your 'no' than a deceitful 'yes'.

I know promises are hard. They require inner strength, integrity, and true work of the heart. I was going to instead ask you to try. But anyone can try. I need you to promise.

14

How To Feel Beautiful When You Feel 50 Shades Of Blurgh

Let's face it—we all have those kind of days. The ones where you don't want to get out of bed, you don't want to face the world, and you don't want to adult. Because for whatever reason, you don't feel good within yourself. And let me tell you, it happens to the best of us. Even those super women whom you think have the world at their feet and this whole life thing figured out.

Yes, even them. So don't go thinking you're on your own with those thoughts, beautiful.

Lucky for you, how you feel is almost entirely up to you. Regardless of what might be happening around you or to you. Life is all about how we choose to see it and what we decide to make of our moments.

Life is about searching for the good, even when it seems like it's not there. Life is about making the most of every single one of your days—because each one of those days is a miracle. Life is about picking yourself up when you're down—because you're far stronger than anything that may be thrown your way.

So here's a little list of pick-me-ups for the next time you find yourself feeling any less than beautiful.

Make a happy playlist.

All of the songs that you can't help but sing out loud to. The ones that make you want to jump up and dance—even when you're in your house all alone. Put a list together of real feel good music—then turn the volume up and let yourself be carried away.

Light some candles and take a bubble bath.

One bath bomb + lit candles + your favourite book + some lovely, relaxing music + a naked you = an hour of pure bliss.

Matching lingerie.

I can't say this enough—wearing a set of gorgeous underwear will make you feel like an unstoppable goddess. Lingerie has super powers like that—try it yourself and see.

Take a trip to the salon.

Having someone else wash and style your hair is the ultimate luxury. Enjoy every minute. And why not try a new look?

Something as simple as getting bangs can make you feel like a new woman.

Read something inspiring.

We live in a time where there is a wealth of inspiring and informative books, blogs, podcasts, and videos created by incredible teachers. All you have to do is look around and envelope yourself in the wisdom, lessons, and powerful messages of hope.

Work out.

Find the one thing that doesn't feel like exercising to you. It might be running, swimming, yogalates, kickboxing, or spinning. Don't stop until you find it, and when you do, don't stop doing it. Working out really does make your body feel good—and looking good is an added bonus.

Think happy thoughts.

Thoughts become things, so think great ones. Think about all of the things that make you feel good. Don't waste any of your precious time on negative ones that bring you down.

Get some fresh air.

Even if going outside and facing the world is the last thing you feel like doing—do it. Moving your body and getting fresh oxygen into your system will help you feel re-energised and ready to conquer the day.

Lipstick is your friend.

Poppy, scarlet, fuchsia, orchid, tango, or orgasm—whatever shade you lust after, make sure it's a BOLD one. You'll be amazed how a bit of bright lippy can transform your entire face and mood.

Compliment someone.

Making others feel good has the power to make you feel all kinds of warm and fuzzy on the inside, too. If you notice something nice about a stranger—tell them. Because who doesn't love receiving a compliment? And the truth is that the more positive energy and love you send out to the world, the more you'll receive back.

Pour yourself a glass of champagne.

This one is inspired by the gorgeous Cara Alwill Leyba and The Champagne Diet. Champagne has way less calories than wine (we're not counting, though!), is far more luxurious, and will make you feel like a queen—even when you feel anything but.

Put on your most fabulous outfit.

While I try not to place too much importance on material possessions, it's amazing what a great outfit can do for your confidence. Lounging around in your sweatpants or pajamas isn't doing you any favours, girl. Get up, get dressed, and get fabulous.

Treat yourself to some fresh flowers.

Don't wait until someone gifts you them—take your life into your own hands, and treat yo'self. Flowers are beautiful to look at and will brighten up your day as well as bring light, energy, and abundance into your whole house.

Indulge in some cocoa.

Because cocoa is magical and has the power to boost your happiness. And it tastes delicious, too.

Write yourself a love letter.

Write down all the things you adore about yourself—all of your accomplishments and triumphs up to now. Celebrate your quirks and flaws—because we all have our own and they make you who you are. When you're done, read your letter back to yourself. Allow your words to sink in to your soul. Feel them and believe them.

Remember you are always in charge of how you feel.

Never, ever forget—you are the only one who holds the power to decide how you feel. Nobody else. Believe in your beauty and you're halfway there.

15

I Will Never Be The Girl Who Believes She Cannot Trust

The trouble with choosing to trust someone is it's like having blind faith. You do it even when common sense is screaming at you not to. You put yourself out there, your head and heart firmly on the chopping block, hoping against all hopes that they're doing the same. That they get it. And they'll be careful with you and your soul. Because that's what you would do. That's what you've always done.

You are the girl who chooses to trust.

But you forget that you are lovely. Sometimes they *won't* be.

Sometimes you will be with someone who can't even begin to understand the fallout of their actions or someone who just selfishly doesn't want to even try. Some people will always be takers, stealing from you silently in the night while giving nothing true in return.

People disappear. They ghost. They cause pain. They cheat.

They leave suddenly and tragically. And sometimes, they just leave.

Label me an eternal optimist, but I don't believe that anybody intentionally sets out to hurt anyone. I think that we wake up each day and face our own demons, whatever shape they choose to take. We do what we believe to be our best. We try. We try to be good people. We fail. We make a mistake. We fall down. Maybe we make a few more mistakes. We struggle. We fight. We might choose to try a little harder. We get back up again. We rinse and repeat.

We know this. But it still hurts like hell when it happens. Why didn't they want to love us? Why couldn't we make them stay?

The thing is that no matter how many times you get hurt, you have to bounce back. You have to realise that they are just one person. One out of a billion others. Know that when your trust is betrayed, it's far more a reflection on that other person than on you and your choice to trust. There are far too many cynical people who never managed to fully recover from their betrayal, who exist as cold shadows of their true selves preferring to now take the easy road because it's familiar and safe and there's less chance of colliding with anybody.

Don't do that. That's not living.

Will it be difficult to pave your way back to the old you? *Of course.* We are creatures who learn from previous events and the consequences or our actions. When we open ourselves fully to someone only to be dumped on the curb and left in a trail of suffocating smoke, we're sure as hell going to do our best to make sure that never happens again. Ever.

But guess what? The new you will be better. You'll have another one of life's invaluable lessons under your wing. You'll be able to trust again, only this time you'll do it with a little more wisdom and care.

I can't tell you how important it is that you don't walk this earth as a jaded shadow of who you once were. Before. Before the worst happened. Before you felt your heart and world shatter and disperse in places so far from where you are right now, you don't believe you'll ever get all of those pieces back again. Don't do that. Don't stop being vulnerable. Don't stop trusting people who are going to walk into your life, before they even do. Being a person who does not trust is being a person who is never fully comfortable with life, always on edge, never at peace.

You must be at peace with yourself.

I won't ever stop being the girl who chooses to trust. She is vulnerable. She is brave. She is kind. She is strong. She is resilient. She believes in good. She believes in people.

She believes in herself.

16

You Are Not Alone

Each morning, I used to walk past a school bus stop on my way to work. And every time, I would take a quick look at the girls stood waiting there, and I'd wonder. I'd wonder about the soft whispering and giggly cliques that I saw and also about the girls standing quietly on their own.

Is everyone in the girl gang happy? Does one of them feel like the weakest link, always being picked on? Is one of them cruel to all the others, but the rest are too afraid to speak up and say something? Out of fear of being cut out of the circle?

Is the girl on her own okay? Does she have her own group of friends she meets once she gets to school? Or does she find herself alone there, too?

School finished ten years ago for me, yet for some reason I *still* can't walk by a group of kids waiting at a bus stop and not think about it. I know it's out of my control, but I feel for them deeply. Maybe it's because I'm really sensitive. Or maybe it's because I used to be that girl standing on her own. Maybe it's both.

I find my eyes filling with tears and my mind filling with what ifs. I just want to go over and stand with them. Ask them if they're okay. Let them know they aren't alone. One in three kids will be the victim of bullying at school, and who knows quite how many will feel like they don't belong. I worry for them because it's so easy as an adult to brush aside their feelings and toss them into the 'it's just part of growing up' bag.

But sometimes it all becomes too much. Sometimes it's one comment, one joke, one punch too many.

If you're one of the girls waiting at the bus stop with your friends, stop and take a look around you next time. Is anyone on their own? Do you know them? Do you not know them? Either way, it doesn't matter. Put yourself in their shoes for a moment—imagine how you might feel

And if you're one of the girls waiting on her own, I want to share a few words with you that have stuck in my mind since the day I heard them as a teenager:

> *The artists, and the scientists, and the poets...none of them fit in at seventeen. You're supposed to get past it. Adults, they see kids killing kids and they know it's a tragedy because they used to be those kids. The bullies and the beaten and the loners. You're supposed to get past it. You're supposed to live long enough to take it back.*
> *— Mouth, One Tree Hill*

You are not the number of friends you have or how popular

you are. You are not how many guys fancy you or how cool your hair or clothes look. And I promise you won't always feel this way. This is merely the *beginning* for you. Your time will come. Never allow cruel words or actions from small minds to bring you down. You are not who they think you are.

Beautiful girl, please know you are most certainly not alone.

17

This Is For The Girls Who Believe There Are No Good Guys Left

I fear people aren't brave anymore. They're afraid to put themselves out there.

We prefer to hide behind a screen and swipe right instead of talking to a stranger. We send meaningless, overthought texts instead of picking up the phone and speaking spontaneously. We endlessly 'hang out' with a bunch of potentials and are scared to put labels on anything. We convince ourselves that being laid back and casual is cool and more attractive than someone who blurts out that they like you too soon.

But it's just not. It's not cool.

Modern dating is tough. Most people can't think of many positive things to say about it. *And I get it.* I often feel cheated by the way that we date now, too. But I don't want you to give up on it just yet. Fight your way through the choppy sea of Netflix & Chill assholes and you'll find a man who wants to take you on actual dates. Sounds improbable at this point, I know. But have faith.

There are still guys out there who want to date you.

They will ask for your number and then call you on the phone. The first time that happens will feel slightly alien but will quickly begin to feel all kinds of lovely. We should all call each other more often.

They will read your messages and reply to them straight away. You won't be left wondering when you'll next hear from them.

Neither of you will be playing a game.

They will arrange to take you out, they will plan and organise, they will put in effort and you'll see it.

They will tell you they've had a great time and they'll mean it. Or they'll respectfully let you know that something doesn't feel quite right for them. They won't cowardly disappear and hope you get their message of stone cold silence.

There are still guys who will open doors for you and will walk on the side of the pavement nearest the traffic. They will tell you that you're beautiful and they'll make you know that you're special; you might not think that you need that right now, but everyone needs that.

On your first date they may or may not kiss you, but they won't try and take any more than that just yet. They won't invite you back to their place. No. They're far too much of a gentleman.

They're in no rush because they're all about the long game. And they're just that into you.

Yes, I promise you that there are still men like this.

They will tell you they want to invest their time in you, only you, and then they will do so. You won't be an option to them. We say that dating a few people at once is normal today. But that's bullshit that we've fed ourselves so we don't feel guilty. They will choose you. And you will know it.

You have to believe it though. You have to believe that guys like this do exist. You have to not settle for residing in a mediocre eternal limbo. You have to be the girl who expects to be treated like she's magic because you are magic.

Believe me when I say there are still guys out there who want to date you.

The world is mostly made up of people who are good, people who want to share their goodness with you.

Please, don't give up on dating just yet.

18

What It Means To Fall In Love Slowly Instead Of Rushing Into Things

I want you to know that it's okay not be the girl who falls fast and hard. It's okay if you're unsure at first and if you don't quite know what to make of your tangle of feelings.

It's okay if you're not sure whether he's the one. And maybe there isn't a 'one.'

We romanticise the hell out of instantly falling head over feels for someone. But in reality, you have no idea who you're falling for. And how could you? How can you know someone after just one date, or one month, or even one year? Truth be told, none of us really know anybody.

We create stories in our heads, and we tell them to ourselves. We paint the picture that we want instead of what we can see. We all chase the fairy tale. We can't help but crave a blockbuster romance. We want to be the Romeo and Juliet, the Jack and

Rose, the Noah and Allie. Always forgetting none of them ever got their happy ending…

Do you know what's great? **Falling slowly.** Slow is sometimes exactly what your heart needs. A break from all the swelling and breaking. Someone who doesn't turn your world upside down. Someone who's going to stick around for a while. Someone who soothes not only your heart, but your soul.

I chose to do something different. I fell for him slowly. The kind of slow where you've been hurt before and you can't help but think it'll happen again if you get yourself too excited about this one. The kind of slow where you're listening to your head as well as your heart. The kind of slow that makes it feel all the more real.

The kind of slow where the butterflies are there but are still, quietly listening, taking every moment in. They were simply preparing to fly.

Many of us are dashing around, blindly reaching out to grab hold of someone. Anyone to help us stand. Because we're scared what will happen when there's no one there and we have to hold our own hand. So we fall hard because all we desperately want is someone to decide to catch us.

Don't let anyone convince you that a slow-starting flame burns any less bright. It might start off slowly, yes. But it's steady. It's not trying to compete. And more often than not, it continues to stay lit long after the instant ones have gone out.

19

14 Life Lessons I Will Absolutely Instill In My Future Daughter

1. Don't worry so much.

About the little things. About the big things. These, too, shall pass. Worrying helps nothing and makes things seem a lot worse than they are in reality. I've found deep breaths, going for a run, and (occasionally) a few glasses of pinot to be helpful.

2. Put your happiness above material stuff.

Make sure that whatever you choose to do with your life it makes you happy and it makes you proud. Money helps with a lot of things and offers a sense of freedom, but it's certainly not everything.

3. Follow your heart.

But always listen to what your head has to say, too. I've found both of these to be important. Don't jump into anything without giving it the full once over. But when it comes down to it, you should always follow what your heart is telling you. It is the path to your soul and it holds the true purpose for your existence in the world.

4. Never stop learning.

Go to school, read books, watch documentaries, take extra classes, talk to people who have different views than you do, talk to people who are older and wiser, spend the money you earn on bettering your mind. Each new day brings with it the opportunity to learn something new, something that you didn't know yesterday. Don't waste it.

5. Be kind, be trustworthy, and have integrity.

I don't believe that anyone is born kind or unkind. It's what we learn as we grow up, from others and our own experiences, and what we choose to allow to shape us. It takes work, practice, and the promise to make good choices today and even better ones the next. You'll also be amazed how rare it is to find these qualities as you grow up. And when people like this come into your life, hold onto them with both hands.

6. Don't ever feel pressured to do anything that you don't want to do.

Those around you will forget about you and that stupid thing you decided to do or not do really quickly, but you won't as easily forget how you betrayed your own moral compass. You will know when something doesn't sit right with you. Don't ignore those feelings; you feel them for a reason.

7. Become the person that you hope to meet.

Whatever you are searching for in a friend or a partner, you need to become that person first. Is it generosity? Is it kindness? Is it intelligence? Is it fearlessness? Whatever it is, work on those qualities within yourself. That's how you'll attract who you're looking for. Like always attracts like.

8. Wait for love.

Try to wait until you're in love before you have sex for the first time. It'll be worth it, I promise. In fact, it's always worth waiting for love. It magnifies every other feeling that there is. Your older self will never be able to thank your younger self enough for being patient.

9. But before you try and love, you need to make sure you love yourself.

I will teach you this from day one, and I will continue to do so, but ultimately it will be up to you to take the torch and carry on ahead. Self-love is the prevalent and purest way to honour and cherish your mind, body, and soul. Without this, your love for others will be hollow, toxic, and unfulfilling. Always try to practice self-love.

10. If you ever find yourself lost and unsure, do not be hesitant to take a different path.

Most people in this world will not be lucky enough to have a crystal clear path mapped out ahead of them. Some of us will have to wander a little and explore farther. Fortune favours the brave. And you must always choose to be brave, especially when you are most fearful, because fear is nothing but an illusion dreamt up in your darkest imagination.

11. Be sure to treat everyone how you hope to be treated.

You will have been told this countless times by now, I'm sure. But it's very important, so listen carefully: People will always remember how you make them feel. Even when you are mistreated, try to look past this, and never lower yourself to someone else's standards.

12. Carbs are not the enemy.

If you feel like a doughnut, have a doughnut, and don't punish yourself for it afterwards. Never deprive yourself of what your body is craving. Listen to it and you will not be steered wrong. A little of everything in moderation is okay. Focus on being healthy, not skinny. Measure yourself in strength and smiles, not in pounds.

13. Expect nothing to ever fall from the sky into your lap.

You have to work very hard in order to be successful. Nothing will happen overnight. It takes perseverance, determination, and the strong mind of a fighter. Keep on relentlessly pushing forward and you will get there one day. Good things will always come to those who work their arses off and never ever give up.

14. Be a flamingo in a flock of pigeons.

It might be difficult to begin with, but each time you choose to do your own thing instead of following the crowd, it will get easier. Be true to who you are and always stand up for what you believe in. Don't be afraid of using your voice to cut through receptions of silence. The world has enough pigeons already.

20

Your Best Is Yet To Come

I've never liked the way some people look back at old photographs or reminisce over distant memories and flippantly say things like, "Those were the best days of my life," or "We had the time of our lives."

No, you *didn't*.

That's only true if you allow it to be your truth. **Your life today and every day after this one will be what you decide it's going to be.** The chances you take, the opportunities you create, and the magic you make for *yourself*.

Your best lives within you, waiting to be found and released. You can't comprehend the potential you hold deep inside. Everything you've ever dreamed of having is just a leap of faith away. Waiting for you to find the courage to say, "I've got this," *and jump*. And every time you make it safely onto higher ground, there will be a step set a little higher above you that you'll instinctively want to reach. **Always go for it.** And this process will continue because your potential and possibility is endless. It knows no bounds and no limits.

Learning to love yourself will be the beginning of the good life you've always dreamed of. The life that never felt within your reach. The life that never seemed like it was meant for you. Self-love will be the start of a sparkly new future. A future you will effortlessly fall in love with.

Don't allow your present worth to be measured by all you have left to accomplish. Don't let any number of unchecked boxes on your life's to-do list determine whether you've succeeded or failed. Don't go thinking it's too late to become the person you always hoped you'd be. And don't go believing that life is a race to the finish line—it's not.

Believe in yourself, and the message you are carrying in your heart. Work hard. *Really* hard. Shoot for the moon. Ignore the haters. Love yourself unapologetically. **Decide who you're going to be in this life and go be *her*.** And it will only be a matter of time before you'll look back on how far you've come and be overwhelmed with pride.

You've got so much left to do here. **You are not done.** Don't think for a second about giving up on yourself. Don't lose hope. Don't stop fighting your inner demons. You've got success to achieve, goals to smash, and dreams to make true. Even if you're struggling to believe in yourself, I want you to know I do. **I believe in you with everything I have.** I know you're going to find your way to some wonderful things. If only you could see it. If only you could see what I see right *now*.

No matter how you might feel about yourself today, always remember that your best days are in *front* of you. **Your best will always be yet to come.** Because there is always room to grow, things to strive for, and the chance to rise up. And most importantly, there will always be space made in your heart to love yourself a little but louder than you did the day before.

21

Don't Fit In If It Hurts

Don't bend and twist yourself to fit into other people's shapes. You have your very own lines, curves, and angles; your outline is just as precious. Don't mess with your mind by drawing comparisons between a circle and a square. Don't mould and manhandle yourself until you're no longer the person you once knew and could've learned to adore.

Don't do anything simply because you *think* you should. And don't allow anyone to convince you you should, either. Don't be afraid to say no to all the things you know won't bring you happiness. And don't be afraid to say yes to the ones that promise to set your soul on fire.

Don't dedicate your life to pleasing others. Don't fall into the trap of striving to make *him* and *her* and *them* proud. Promise me you'll always make yourself proud first, okay? Go your own way. Pave a new path. Because this is your life, and you must fill it with the colour, beauty, and music that will make your heart sing.

Don't let anyone tell you who you are or who you might

become. Because that is all still up to you. Don't let yourself be steered off the path you know you're meant to take. Don't pay attention to idle gossip and toxic whispers. And don't allow whatever happens to you in this life to change you. To label you. Or damage you. Because you are so much stronger than any of the challenges thrown your way.

Don't say you're sorry when you're not. Don't give out your apologies when too many are still waiting and owed to you. Don't pardon the person you are. Not your thoughts, your choices, or your actions. Don't shrink yourself down to cater to other people's egos. Don't spend your life *excusing* yourself.

Don't try and fake a smile when you're hurting. When tears are flooding your insides. Don't pretend you're okay when you're crying on the floor. Don't think you always have to be this strong, unbreakable woman. Don't think your pain needs to be shadowed because that pain makes you human. That pain makes you an un-edited picture of raw beauty.

Don't be afraid of goodbyes. Don't be afraid to leave if you've outgrown your space and the people who once filled it up. Don't endlessly give the best parts of your soul to those who give you nothing but heartache in return. Don't be afraid to walk out on someone who treats you badly and doesn't alight your sparkle. And don't be afraid to never look back. Because the past can never help you move forward.

And don't try to fit in if it hurts. Because it shouldn't. Don't collect bruises and scars and confuse them as badges of honour. Don't wear those battle wounds proudly because in time, you'll see they've cut you deeper than you thought. Don't let those cuts run too deep or else soon enough you won't recognise who you are. Don't fit in if it hurts. Because I promise you *it's not supposed to hurt*. If something ever stings your heart, it's a sign from the universe warning you *this is not meant for you.*

22

This Is For The Girls Who Are Hard Work To Love

Once upon a time, you probably dated, or maybe you're still dating, a guy who has told you that you're difficult. Challenging. High maintenance. Stubborn AF. *Hard work.* I hope you didn't take it as criticism. I hope you took it as a compliment. Because it is one.

Word on the street is I'm hard work, but you know what? **I think all the best girls are.**

We expect to date in the old-fashioned sense of the word. He has to make a noticeable effort. The first date is his one chance to make a bold first impression. We want him to sweep us off our feet. Of course we do. But what girl doesn't?

We keep guys on their toes. There's no room for them to grow complacent. They have to continue to impress us long after the initial dating game is over.

We're strongly opinionated. But it's only because we care so deeply about a whole lot of things—even those far beyond our control.

We call guys out on their bullshit. Because we quickly recognise when we're not being treated the way we deserve to be. And maybe no one else has the balls to tell him he's being an asshole. But we'll step up. Not because we like pointing the finger. Not because we revel in conflict. Not because we want to gain the upper hand. But because our hearts always push us into doing what our heads know is right.

It's not always easy, but we will do it anyway.

He might tell you you're hard work, but girls like us never label ourselves easy.

If they let us down, they soon expect to hear about it. And why shouldn't they? Keeping quiet when someone you care about has caused you pain, is only going to give that pain room to linger and grow.

We expect a lot. We want someone in their entirety. Their time. Their mind. Their affection. Their heart. And we want to see their soul too.

Okay, so we might want the world.

But we'll offer the world, too.

That's why he stuck around so long. That's why he hasn't let you go.

We challenge someone to be their best self, just like we challenge ourselves. We expect the best because we know just how good they have the capacity to be. We've seen him be better, so we find ourselves unable to accept less.

We fight to the end of the earth for someone and all the way back again. Because nowhere is too far. **And he will always be worth it.**

We will be there for them, always. Through the sunshine and thunderstorms. Especially those thunderstorms. Because life is hard, and love can be even harder. But it's also the only thing that manages to pull us through sometimes.

We love like no one else does.

Fiercely. Completely. Unapologetically. We will give somebody our everything.

Call us hard work, but all we're ever asking for is the same in return.

23

In A World Full Of 'Look At Me' Girls, Be A 'Come With Me' Girl

We live in a world crowded with people who crave attention and validation. A line up of girls waiting to do *whatever* it takes to get picked for the latest reality TV shit-show. Because who cares about dignity and grace when there's 10k up for grabs, right? Posting incessant streams of selfies in the hopes of having people adore their edited and improved selves. Because you're only ever the amount of likes, comments, and followers you have, right? Striving to be the popular girl—the one with the most friends, and the one who *always* gets the guy she wants, no matter who else he might have his eye on. Because the biggest cheer squad + a hot piece of arm candy = **#priorities**, right?

We live in a world full of 'look at me' girls. Girls who have totally lost sight of what used to matter to them most. Before the world got in their head. Before those voices crept in their ears. Before they cashed in and let go of their *real* dreams for a diluted version of success.

In a world full of girls pleading that you look at them, dare to be different. **Be a girl who invites the world to come *with* her.**

Leave your agenda behind you. You don't need one. Do things simply because of the joy they bring you and not for what you might personally gain. And while you're at it, you can leave behind the picture of the woman you think you *need* to be in order to be liked. You don't need to be, do, or say anything that doesn't stay true to who you are at your centre.

Just be generous with your time and your means, be selfless from your heart with your intentions, and be kind in your actions and your words. Because there isn't a whole lot else that matters quite like these things do.

Create something meaningful and with purpose. Start a movement, help people, invoke real change, exchange your time for something you will be able to look back on in ten years and still swell with pride at the memory of.

Remember, it is *your* choice how you spend the rest of your life.

Don't rely on your body or your looks to take you where you want to go. Trust that your heart and your mind are far more powerful than anything physical. Set an example to anyone who might be watching and admiring you from the sidelines. Strive to be the kind of role model you hope your daughter one day has in her life to look up to. The kind of role model maybe you lacked and wished you had.

Realise you are so much stronger when you stand together with other women, lifting each other up. Don't try to compete. You are in your own competition, and it's a competition for *one*. Lead from the front and extend your hands to bring others along with you on this shared journey. Because what this world needs is more girls who genuinely want to link arms and take it on *together*.

24

The Art Of Loving Yourself

You yourself, as much as anybody in the entire universe, deserve your love and affection.
—Buddha

Why is it that we can fall head over heels in love with a perfect stranger in a heartbeat, yet when it comes to loving ourselves, we can endlessly struggle?

Self-love is something I personally battled with for the majority of my teens and early twenties. I was uncomfortable in my own skin. I couldn't help but compare myself to all the girls I encountered daily and believed were prettier, smarter, and more popular than me. I often wished I could wake up as somebody else. *Anybody* else.

And it breaks my heart that I just wrote that. I wouldn't wish that feeling on anyone.

Today, you'll be met with a bubbly, positive, and confident

young woman. But the journey to get to where I find myself now has not been an easy one. I didn't wake up one day and miraculously feel like an unstoppable goddess. It took *years* of changing bad habits, practising new ones, confronting my fears, and learning to believe in myself no matter what.

I want you to know that if I can learn to love myself, I believe with all my heart that you can, too.

And you *must.*

Realise that you are enough.

The trouble is that you're so used to being *you* that you can't see yourself the way that the rest of the world sees you. You are lovely, and you are kind. You are smart, you are funny, you are brave, and you are brilliant. You are magic, and you are raw beauty.

Wherever you may be as you read this, I want you to know that you are *enough.* Contrary to what the world and your inner demons might have you believe, you are so much more than enough.

Forgive yourself and others.

We all make mistakes, so quit being so hard on yourself. Mistakes are a valuable way to learn and grow—so please, make plenty.

We are all simply human beings navigating this crazy thing called life.

Learn to forgive others who have hurt you and caused you pain. When you forgive, you allow your heart to let go of the pain that you are carrying around with you—and it does not belong there. Make room for more love.

Do what makes your heart happy.

We only get one shot at living our lives. One chance, one opportunity to make a difference, chase our dreams, and write an incredible legacy.

Ten years from now, you won't look back and be happy that you stayed in your unfulfilling 9-5 job, that you said no to exploring the world, or that you didn't at least try and turn your dreams into a reality. Ten years from now, you'll wish you started living the life you've always imagined *today.*

Understand that nobody is perfect.

Everyone has their own battles, their own struggles, and their own demons that they are waking up to each day and fighting. On the surface, you might think that somebody has the perfect life—success, money, and love—but the truth is, you don't know them. You don't know the journey they have been on to get where they are now, and you don't know what they might be facing right now.

Nobody is perfect, and the perfect life does not exist. The day you realise this is the day you will stop punishing yourself for not living up to impossible ideas of perfection.

Stop looking for love externally.

Don't look for love in a friend or a partner before you have learned to love yourself. Because nobody is meant to complete you. You are meant to be whole on your own.

If you're not quite there yet, don't worry. It will take months, maybe even years of changing your current beliefs.

If ever you are in need of love, look within you. Everything you could ever need has been waiting patiently in your heart all along.

Tell yourself you're beautiful.

Wherever you might be right now—find a mirror in your handbag, on your wall, or even on your phone. Study the person staring back at you. Think of everything you've been through that has led you to this moment. Think of all your accomplishments, your successes, and your fondest memories. Think about everything you've faced and overcome. Think about all of the things that you like about yourself. All of the qualities that make you so incredibly special.

Wherever you might be right now, I want you to look in to the nearest mirror and say, "I am beautiful." Say it more than once, say it over and over; shout it, sing it, embody it.

Practise gratitude.

Do you have any idea how amazing it is right now that you are *alive*? That you are able to be here reading this? Probably not because the real chances of you being here are so incredibly minute we cannot begin to fathom them.

You might be having a bad day, a bad week, or even a bad *year.* But life is merely how you decide to look at it. Choose to practise gratitude. Be thankful for all of the wonderful things you have instead of wasting time thinking about what you don't.

Find your tribe.

Don't worry if you haven't found them yet; I promise you that your tribe is out there. Stop spending time with people who aren't making you truly happy merely to make up the numbers.

Spend time with positive people. People who challenge and inspire you to be better each day. People who will always tell you the truth, even when it's hard. People who are kind and selfless. People who will lift you *up.*

When you surround yourself with kind and loving spirits, those thoughts, feelings, and energy will transfer to you.

Stop being so hard on yourself.

You're doing better than you think you are. I promise you that.

If you want to do and be better, great. Start now. But don't beat yourself up for what you yet managed to achieve. Focus on everything that you have done well. Everything that makes you proud to be *you*.

Take yourself on a date.

So what if you don't have a romantic partner right now? So what if you do? There is no better way to show yourself some much needed attention and love than to plan and take yourself out on a solo date. Enjoy a fabulous candle-lit dinner alone with a good book or simply your thoughts. Pack a picnic full of your favourite eats and treats and savour it in a pretty park. Go and see that movie that nobody wants to see and love every moment of it.

Don't be afraid of your own company. Spending quality time with yourself is the best way to begin and strengthen your self-love journey.

Reflect.

Even if you don't love writing, spend regular time journaling and daydreaming. Reflect on your days, what went well, and what you want to improve on. You will begin to notice patterns in the way you think and behave. Once you know what these patterns are, you will be able to understand more about the person you are and why you are that way.

If self-love is something you struggle with, this will pinpoint why and where you are struggling so you can begin to overcome this.

Honour and cherish who you are.

> *Remember always that you not only have the right to be an individual, you have an obligation to be one.*
> *—Eleanor Roosevelt*

Don't try and change the real you in order to fit into other people's skewed views of what is 'normal', 'acceptable', or 'beautiful'. You are you, and you are beautiful. Never let the world dull your sparkle. Your soul will shine brightest in its natural form.

You do you. Forget everyone else. The sooner you realise that you are here on earth do something utterly unique, the sooner you will learn to celebrate your differences.

25

This Is The Kind Of Love You Deserve

You deserve someone who wants to give you a fucking text back, you know? Someone who wants you, only you, and makes you *feel* wanted. Someone who can't help but message you first thing in the morning when the sunlight is slow-dancing through the curtain and they're barely waking. Someone who wants to spend their drunken Friday nights with you but also their lazy lemonade Sundays. Someone who holds their one-person umbrella right above you when the rain is bucketing down so that you're sheltered, even if it means they get soaked through. You deserve someone who thinks of you often. Someone who calls you on the phone at the end of a long day because they want to hear the sound of your voice before they drift off into slumber. Someone who makes plans with you on a Tuesday evening because the weekend is just too far away—and who cares if we have to go to work the next day? **Someone who says *definitely*, not *maybe*, and follows through.** You deserve to hear a song on the radio that makes you melt on the inside at the mere thought of this someone.

Someone who could watch you sleeping for hours at a time and be perfectly content in the grace and stillness of that moment. Someone who steals a cheeky kiss when you're mid-sentence and least expecting to find their lips. Someone who will happily pig out on pizza with you in bed and not judge the sweat-pants and top knot look you're sporting. Someone who is just that into you. You deserve someone who challenges the both of you constantly—someone who makes you strive to be better each day because they're trying to be better, too. Someone you can count on to stick around when the shit hits the fan (which it *will*). Someone who chooses to lift you up always. You deserve magic, fireworks, and confetti canons exploding in your clear blue skies. You deserve someone who will always be careful with your heart because they know just how fragile it already was before they held it. Someone whose heart aches whenever yours does. Someone who wakes up next to you each day feeling like they've hit the jackpot over and over again and thinks what on earth did they do in their past life to be so damn lucky? You deserve someone's complete attention. **Someone who looks at you, and I mean *really* sees you, and all of the beauty you hold.** You deserve to be someone's first choice. Someone's best friend. Someone's partner in crime. Someone's everything. You deserve to be loved; loved extraordinarily well. And to be told that you are loved every single day.

Beautiful girl, you deserve no less than this kind of love.

26

To The Girl I Used To Be

To the girl I used to be: I'm sorry.

My heart still shares your pain. I'm sorry you never felt like you belonged. For all those times you let others tell you who you were and push you around. I'm sorry you never believed in your voice or found your inner strength. Maybe you were searching but couldn't find it. And maybe you were never meant to just yet. I'm sorry you saw your pain as a burden and that you didn't have anybody to comfort you. I'm sorry you felt utterly unlovable and alone.

To the girl I used to be: you're barely recognisable.

Scared, timid, sad, lonely, afraid, unsure, and oh-so helpless—it's time I bid you farewell. It's time to finally let go of your hands. Because the truth is she was never who I truly am at heart. She was the product of other people's thoughts, opinions, and wishes. She was not herself. She was a shadow of the reflection I see today.

To the girl I used to be: I wish you could've known what I do now.

You don't know it yet, you're blissfully unaware, but you're incredible. You are kind to strangers. You always listen to other's worries and take them on as if they were your own. You are loyal. Fiercely so. You're sweet and you're thoughtful. You can't help but think of others because that's who you are. You're all kinds of lovely. And you are smart. Smarter than you allow yourself to believe. And so very talented. You're beautiful, too. Oh yes, you are. They might not see it; you might not see it, but it's within you. It always has been.

And I hope the world gets to see all of you some day.

To the girl I used to be: thank you.

Thank you for not giving up even when you couldn't see the light. Thank you for striving to be better. For finding a way. Thank you for shaping me into the strong, courageous woman I am today. Thank you for finally realising that the ticket to a better life was in your hands all along. Thank you for choosing to love and to live.

To the girl I used to be: if only you could see me now.

Happy, strong, powerful, brave, confident, blessed, and head-over-heels in love with life. The kind of woman that would make my younger self incredibly proud. The kind of woman I always dreamed of becoming.

To the girl I used to be: this is finally goodbye.

27

I Am Enough

Dear Self,

Hey, you. Yes, you. Listen up, soul sister. You are powerful beyond measure. And more beautiful than you could even begin to imagine right now.

Newsflash, girl: You are a total GODDESS.

Oh yes, you *are*.

Now repeat after me:

From today, **I promise to stop being so damn hard on myself.** I promise to make my mistakes but never allow them to make *me*. Because I am only human. And I'm a pretty awesome one. As good as a spoonful of Nutella right out the jar, or taking your bra off at the end of a long-ass day, or treating yourself to ice cream topped with rainbow sprinkles for breakfast. When I'm having a rough day, I'll spare a little thought for everyone else out there. All of those hearts swelling and breaking. I'll remind myself of everything I have to be grateful for. And I'll play my happy song on repeat until it takes me there. Because life is too short to give too many precious days away to those blues.

I promise to love and respect my body. To not wish I was curvier, thinner, taller, smaller, tanned, or fairer. I will focus on all of the ways in which my beautiful body allows me to live a rich and rewarding life. I will no longer punish myself for wanting or eating that slice of triple chocolate cake. Because cake is delicious and is not the enemy. From now on, I promise to listen to my body and what it craves. Because a little bit of everything does me no harm. And what would life be without cake? **I promise to instead focus on the parts of myself I *adore*.** All of my qualities and quirks. Because they make me who I am. And that girl is *beautiful*. I will banish the negative thought that just crept into my mind, telling me I'm not good enough. Because it's wrong. It was wrong yesterday, and it will be just as wrong tomorrow. And if ever those voices come back—I will shut them the fuck down. They hold no power over me.

I will love myself today and every day after. With all that I have. Even if I'm struggling to feel it, I will say it. I will look at that girl staring back at me in the mirror. And I will repeat those three words until they are my *truth*. I will allow my soul to sparkle exactly as it is. Because the world *needs* my magic in it.

No matter where life takes me. No matter what is thrown my way. And no matter what they may say. The only person in charge of the way I feel about myself is *me*. I am love and I am light. I own my worth. And I am *worthy*. Of Abundance.

Happiness. Prosperity. Kindness. Good fortune. Loving relationships. Grand adventure. And the marvel of miracles.

Every day after this one, I promise to remember this:

I AM ENOUGH.

All my love,

Me

28

Bloom

Bloom where you're planted.

Where your roots belong and your beginnings began.

You need not travel far or wide to find your way to the light.

Just aim upwards. Stand as tall as you can.

You will see that even the rain is on your side.

Feel your petals grow restless as you become sure of what you hold within.

As you grow in confidence and soak up the sunlight.

Allow your true colours to burst open from their bud, showering your magic.

Bloom and blossom

Into the beautiful flower you were always destined to become.

About the Author

Shani is a writer, author, and self-love advocate. She runs her own content creation business based in the UK. She is the founder of The Glow Getter Tribe–shanijay.com/glowgetter–a self-love and kindness movement which helps young girls and women worldwide feel happy, confident, and beautiful starting from the inside, out. You can join her mission today on Instagram @shanijaywriter and get some glow, too!

YOU MIGHT ALSO LIKE:

You Are Enough
by Becca Martin

All The Words I Should Have Said
by Rania Naim

This Is The Love You Deserve
by Thought Catalog

THOUGHT CATALOG Books

THOUGHT CATALOG

IT'S A WEBSITE.

www.thoughtcatalog.com

SOCIAL

facebook.com/thoughtcatalog
twitter.com/thoughtcatalog
tumblr.com/thoughtcatalog
instagram.com/thoughtcatalog

CORPORATE

www.thought.is

CPSIA information can be obtained
at www.ICGtesting.com
Printed in the USA
BVHW041233190522
637508BV00007B/223

9 781945 796524